BREAKING FREE
FROM PARTNER ABUSE

Also by Mary Marecek:

Let Go of Guilt
(Boston: Red Sun Press)

Jane Roberts' A View from the Other Side
(Sedona, Arizona: Light Technology Publishing)

BREAKING FREE
FROM
PARTNER ABUSE

Voices of Battered Women
Caught in the Cycle
of Domestic Violence

By Mary Marecek
Illustrated by Jami Moffett

Morning
Glory
Press

Buena Park, California

Library of Congress Cataloging-in-Publication Data

Marecek, Mary.
    Breaking free from partner abuse : voices of battered women
caught in the cycle of domestic violence / by Mary Marecek;
illustrated by Jami Moffett.
    96 p. cm.
    Includes bibliographical references.
    ISBN 1-885356-57-9 $15.95 (cloth) : 1-885356-53-6
$8.95 (pbk.)
    1. Wife abuse. 2. Wife abuse--United States. I Title.
HV6626.M34   1999
    362.82'92--dc21   98-44933
                                                    CIP

MORNING GLORY PRESS, INC.
6595 San Haroldo Way   Buena Park, CA 90620-3748
(714) 828-1998
Printed and bound in the United States of America

Contents

Abuse is all the physical, emotional, or psychological actions or threats of action that influence power, control, or force over another human being. This includes anything that frightens, intimidates, terrorizes, manipulates, hurts, humiliates, blames, injures, or wounds.

Acknowledgments

Thank you—To the hundreds of women who have shared their stories: Latina, African American, Portuguese, Asian, Ethiopian, Indian, German, Hungarian, Irish, English, Italian, Native American, Haitian, and Anglo. Thanks also to the lesbians among you who took the risk, and broke the conspiracy of silence. This is for all of you so you can hear each others' voices. Thank you for sharing your past, your present, and your hopes for the future.

All your names have been changed to protect your identities since many of you still live in fear, need protection, and are not free from violence in your lives.

Foreword

One-third to one-half of all American women are, at some time, beaten by their husbands or lovers. Somewhere in the United States a woman is beaten every 18 seconds.

When I was working on the *Teenage Couples Series,* more than 3700 teenagers responded to a survey of their attitudes toward marriage and relationships. Almost one-sixth of the teenage women and one-fifth of the teenage men said it was okay for a husband to hit his wife, or sometimes it's necessary, or it may happen when he's angry or drunk. Nearly twice as many boys as girls said, "It's not good but sometimes it's necessary." In other words, two out of ten boys didn't see anything much wrong in men hitting women.

People are *not* for hitting, whether male or female. The problem is much more severe for women, however, simply because of their size and strength as compared to men. In most situations, the man is bigger and can hit harder than the woman. From a physical standpoint, if she hits him, he can stop her. But she can't stop him.

If a big kid hits a little kid, we call him a bully. Most of us would consider such an act wrong. Big kids aren't supposed to beat up little kids.

Then why does such a big part of our population apparently think it's okay for a man to beat up a woman as long as she is his wife or girlfriend?

A group of psychology students didn't believe their college professor when he told them that many people in our society think it's perfectly all right for a man to hit his wife or girlfriend. They decided to perform an experiment to prove him wrong.

They developed three skits which they acted out in a busy shopping center. First, two young men staged a fight. Passersby stopped the skirmish immediately. Then two young women started beating on each other. Again, people walking by stopped them. The final skit was a man beating a woman. Nobody interfered. Instead, they made comments such as "It's probably his wife," "I'll bet she deserves it," and "I wonder what she did to get herself in that situation."

The students couldn't believe it. So they repeated their experiment several times. Each time, the results were the same. If the hitting is within the family, we mustn't interfere. We act as if the marriage license is a hitting license!

A person who feels guilty herself because her husband hit her is not likely to leave him. She doesn't feel good enough about herself to be able to take that step. Often the biggest problem is dealing with one's own guilt. She feels embarrassed, damaged. She thinks she must have done something wrong. Or if she didn't do something wrong, she must *not* have done something she was supposed to do.

Suzanne explained why she stayed with her husband for more than a year even though he beat her:

> *Everybody says, "If my husband ever hit me, I would leave." Well, it's not that easy. I thought I brought it on myself. I would hit him back, but I was always careful not to hurt him. He didn't care if he hurt me. He hit hard.*
>
> *I always thought it was my fault, that I caused it. I called him names or I pushed him until I made him mad enough to hit me. But now I realize there's almost nothing you can do that is cause for that.*
>
> *I finally realized he had problems, that he was really sick, and it wasn't my fault. It wasn't because he hated me or even disliked me — he really loved me. I think it had a lot to do with his parents, with his dad beating him, and his mom and dad fighting. I finally realized it wasn't me, and I left.*
>
> (Suzanne, married at 17 to Bill, 19)

I have worked with pregnant and parenting teens for 25 years, and I've talked with many young women who have been abused by their partners. Partner abuse is a problem for women of all ages, but even more so for teenage women. A young woman who hasn't yet found her self-identity, especially if early pregnancy and parenting reinforce her feelings of dependence, may be a prime target for an abusive partner relationship.

When I was teaching, students occasionally explained

their absence from class by saying they didn't want the other girls to see them with a black eye.

One day we were showing the video, "The Burning Bed," in class. About half-way through the movie, a student rushed out of the classroom in tears. I followed her, knowing her partner was abusive, and concerned that the movie had made her feel even worse.

As she stood outside crying, she said, "They think it's easy to leave. They just don't understand. I can't leave him . . ." She had heard a couple of the other students talking about her situation, and she simply couldn't handle it.

If you have a friend who is being abused by her partner, you probably wonder why she doesn't leave him. But, whatever your age, if you're the victim of abuse, you *know* how hard it is to walk out, to face life on your own. You may think you deserve the abuse, which makes it even harder to get out.

In *Breaking Free from Partner Abuse,* Mary Marecek shares the stories of women caught in this dilemma, women who can't find a way to leave an abusive partner. She also shares accounts of women who finally manage to get out and go on with their lives, free of abuse.

These personal accounts combined with Marecek's poetry and her compassionate, realistic, and encouraging suggestions can help an abused woman find the strength to leave her abuser. That's what this book is all about.

Jeanne Warren Lindsay, Author
Teenage Couples: Caring, Commitment and Change
Teenage Couples: Coping with Reality
Teenage Couples: Expectations and Reality

October, 1998

To the many women
who have endured abuse,
and who have shared their hopes,
their pain,
and their dreams with me.

It's time to recognize the violence, put a stop to it.

Introduction

How often have you gasped in disbelief as your husband tore the phone off the wall? Stared in silence while he verbally attacked you for things you didn't do? Shook uncontrollably after being pushed and shoved around?

Do you know what it means if he suddenly hits you across the face, says you're no good, that you've been messing around with another man, that you can't go to the store, talk on the phone, go out with friends?

Well, it's time to recognize the violence,
put a stop to it
feel safe and
start all over again.

You deserve a life without violence!

We live in an environment of violence. It is all around us. The daily newspaper, the nightly news attest to the fact that our world is at war with itself: murder, rape, muggings, child abuse, and wife beatings. Living in an insecure world where basic needs are not met fosters fear, frustration, and, ultimately, violence. "Might makes right," "Power prevails," and "A gun will make you safe" are a few of the clichés that encourage violence.

You can't change others. You *can* change yourself. You can't keep an abuser from abusing. You *can* make certain you are not the victim of the abuse.

Get away. Leave. Find a safe place to stay. These are things you can do: Take charge. Make decisions. Move. Don't wait to be acted upon. Act. Don't wait for things to get better. They won't. Violence only gets worse. Hope can get you killed. Your only hope is yourself.

We received a call from a shelter on Cape Cod asking if we had room for a woman who had been badly beaten. We did, and she came up to Boston. Carla had bruises all over her body, burns on her thighs and buttocks, and her broken arm was so swollen it couldn't be set. She stayed with us for a few days, and then returned to her husband. As she left, she said she was going back because she missed him.

Two years later we read about her in the Boston Globe. She had shot and killed her husband. Her history of abuse and the many hospital records were proof of the tormented life she lived, and she was not indicted.

In Carla's case, hope could have gotten her killed. In her case, it didn't kill her; it killed her husband.

i whisper to the wind

i whisper to the wind, "he beats me"
i say a prayer at night that he will go
i dare not speak the truth to others
my family, friends and children: they all know

they all whisper to the wind, "he beats her"
they say a prayer at night that he will go
they dare not speak the truth to others
their family, friends and children: they all know

we've created a conspiracy of silence
no one tells the other what she knows
we all whisper to the wind, "he beats her"
and say a prayer at night that he will go

I am defeated woman . . .

despair

Once I could get angry with you
And my arrogance felt good
I'd rant and rave justified
You weren't treating me like you should.

Now my anger is at myself
For staying with you so long
My anger has turned inward
And the depression lasts so long.

I don't get angry anymore
I cringe and cower and shake
I fear your every movement
Your words can make me break.

I am defeated woman
Not proud of me or you
I am the battered woman
A crushed and worn-out shoe.

the encounter

it was an encounter of the near-death kind:

i left my body

i detached and looked around

saw nothing, was nothing

was safe in the beyond.

when i came back you stood over me

clenched fists, bloodied hands

back in my body i felt the hurt of your hits

my swollen face looked back at me in the mirror

sore ribs convinced me you had kicked me

i wouldn't have known: i wasn't there

while you were breaking up my body

i had left you:

it was an encounter of the near-death kind.

You Don't Deserve Abuse

ONE

No one deserves to:

1. Be pushed, shoved, pounded, slapped, bruised, kicked, or strangled.

2. Be verbally attacked or accused.

3. Have possessions damaged.

4. Be interfered with in comings and goings.

5. Be ridiculed, put down, made fun of, or belittled (alone or in front of others).

6. Be followed, harassed, or spied on.

7. Be emotionally starved.

8. Be isolated.

So often when we talk with abused women about their rights, they say, "I didn't know I could do that," or "If only I had known years ago that I didn't have to put up with that."

Shirley came to our shelter from New York. She lived with an abusive husband who was the head of a Mental Health Agency.

"I didn't know that I could leave him," she said. "He left me. No one believed me when I told them about the abuse. He's a pillar in this community, and he's well-liked by everyone. I was brought up Catholic so it never occurred to me that I could leave him.

"When I think of all the beatings and verbal abuse I took for six years, I know I must have been crazy to stay. I just didn't know I had the right to leave."

1. No one deserves to

Be pushed, shoved, pounded, slapped, bruised, kicked or strangled. No one. There is no excuse that makes it tolerable. Not alcohol, not unemployment, not financial problems, not family patterns, not sickness, not children, not stress.

There are no reasons that make it okay.

*"He wouldn't hit me if he didn't drink," Kay told
me during a counseling session.*

*"I know he loves me. He's always sorry after it's
over, and he never remembers what he did. If only
he didn't drink."*

*Kay returned, still hoping the abuse would stop,
still protecting him, still making excuses for him.*

It didn't stop.

2. No one deserves to

Be attacked verbally: accused of things you don't do,
called names, yelled at for no apparent reason, lied to, or
have your reality denied.

*Elizabeth has two master's degrees. When she
came in for counseling, she looked disoriented. It
was hard to picture her teaching college students.
She was having difficulty distinguishing between
fact and fiction.*

*"My husband denies what I know to be the
truth," she said. "I paid for the car, and he says he
paid for it."*

*She recounted many incidents of him denying her
reality and telling her to call his mother or his
brother if she didn't believe him.*

*She was confused, and was starting to doubt her
own sense of reality.*

*Elizabeth and I talked for several weeks, and
then she just stopped coming to sessions. The last I
heard she was teaching part-time at a nearby
college.*

*I don't know what she's doing to maintain her
own sense of reality or her sanity.*

3. No one deserves to

Have possessions damaged: dishes thrown, clothes torn, radio smashed. Things bought together do not automatically become "his" just because he paid for them from joint money. And you are not one of his possessions.

> *I took Maureen back to her apartment to pick up her possessions after she had been at the shelter for the weekend. We followed regular procedure: when we were within two blocks of the house, we called the police. They met us and entered the apartment with us. Her drunken husband refused to give her anything, shouting that everything was his.*
>
> *The police convinced him he should let her have her own clothes, and we found them hidden in the garage. After twenty years of marriage, Maureen left with five bags of clothes.*

4. No one deserves to

Be interfered with in comings and goings. You do not need to be told when you can or cannot leave the house, shop, go back to school.

> *Yolanda is in her late teens. During a support group session, she told a horror story of being locked in the house every day with the door bolted and bars on the windows. Her lover had virtually made a prisoner of her. She was not allowed to talk on the telephone, go to the store, talk to the neighbors, or go anywhere without him.*
>
> *He assured her that it was for her own good—he didn't want her to get mugged or raped out on the*

street. She didn't realize the psychotic nature of his behavior until she was his prisoner.

Yolanda escaped one morning and came to the shelter. She lives in terror that he will find her and imprison her again.

5. No one deserves to

Be followed, harassed, or spied on. You have the right to go where you want, spend time where you choose, without interference.

Debbie came to us from the Midwest. She had been followed, spied on, and harassed at home and at work even after she divorced her husband. She didn't feel safe until she put a thousand miles between herself and her abuser. She says she still looks over her shoulder in fear that he will find her, and that she will only feel safe again when he is dead.

6. No one deserves to

Be ridiculed, put down, made fun of, or belittled, alone or in front of others. Years of seeing others forced to accept ridicule by men in both overt and covert ways make it seem reasonable to accept ridicule, but we must never become resigned to it. We must see it for the form of disrespect it really is, and understand that it will escalate into violence.

When Mollie came in for counseling, she said she had been married for thirty-three years. She had experienced physical, verbal, emotional, and

No one deserves to be isolated.

sexual abuse all those years. The worst, she said,
was the ridicule and the put-downs of her in front
of her two grown sons and her father who lived
with them.

"I can take anything," she said, "but the ridicule
is the worst."

Mollie talks of moving out, and has seen a
lawyer about a divorce, but to date, she is still there
suffering the abuse. Thirty-three years is a long
time. Changing is not easy. For some, it is
impossible.

7. No one deserves to

Be emotionally starved. Everyone has emotional needs:
to love, to be loved, to care and be cared for, to need
others and to be needed by others. It takes many people
to meet one person's needs. If your focus is only on
a husband or lover, you may be starved for affection
and attention.

Connie said during a session, "I don't know who
I am or what I want. I only know myself in relation
to my ex, or to Jim, or to my sons. I'm afraid of
making a choice to get a job or to go to school. I
might make a mistake." Tears trickled down her
cheeks.

"Be patient with yourself; be good to yourself.
There's no such thing as a mistake, just another
way of doing something," I said. She smiled.

"Take some time to get centered, time for your-
self," I continued. "Until you spend some time with
yourself, you won't know who you are. Once you

*get some confidence in yourself, you'll know better
what it is you want to do."*

*Connie is pleased that she's beginning to ques-
tion her own behavior. "It's a step," I said, "a
baby step, and baby steps become giant steps, and
giant steps become self-confidence, and self-
confidence becomes positive self-image, and
positive self-images can change your world."*

8. No one deserves to

Be isolated. No woman is an island, and living as if you
are one will lead to crisis. Unless you're a Tibetan monk,
you need others in your life.

*Cheryl divorced her first husband after six years
of abuse and harassment. Her second husband
proved to be much the same. She is growing in
awareness though: when he suggested they move to
rural Massachusetts where she would be ten miles
from the nearest town, without a car or a tele-
phone, she got suspicious. "Why would he want to
isolate me that way?" she asked.*

*She started listening more closely to his words
and observing his actions, and found him to be
violent, bigoted, possessive, and having a great
need to control her actions. Soon after our session,
she asked him to leave.*

*Now Cheryl is trying to raise her two sons by
herself. It's difficult to build up a support system
and be a single parent, but she's determined. She
doesn't want to be isolated nor live with an abuser
again. She's hoping to do better this time.*

Cheryl is only twenty-seven. She may make it.

hope

After you once raised your voice to me
Then your hand
Then your fist
I lost respect
    for you
    for myself
    for us . . . what we once were
And never will be again.

I live in hope
    that you will change
    that I won't feel guilty
    that we will be happy
    that you will stop drinking
    that you will die.

My hope is a pipe-dream
I live in hope.

understanding

I'm beginning to understand

the horror of my situation
the bleakness of my life
the emptiness of my future
cuts me like a knife.

I'm beginning to understand

the madness of who you are
the hollowness of day
the sadness of the fighting
what else can I say?

I'm beginning to understand

the joke life played on me
how futile are my dreams
the absence of my anger
the silence of my screams.

You Have
the Right

You have the right to:

1. Be treated with respect.

2. Be heard.

3. Say "No."

4. Come and go as you please.

5. Have a support system.

6. Have friends and be social.

7. Have privacy and space of your own.

8. Maintain a separate identity.

1. You have the right to

Be treated with respect. Regardless of life-style, economic standing, religion, race, or sex, we all have this right. Respect means absence of violence and acknowledgment as human beings.

Mary Fran is divorced, and she says she was having trouble with her two children, ages eleven and nine. She was feeling extremely angry and couldn't figure out why. She described a typical day. She told how the children talked to her, and how she finally realized they were being disrespectful. The underlying message in their daily interactions was a lack of respect for Mary Fran.

"They like me and they love me, but I don't feel respected. It's making me feel angry and resentful toward them. I don't even want to kiss them good night," she said.

Once Mary Fran realized that the problem was a lack of respect for her, she was able to work with the children on setting limits and boundaries. She's feeling better about herself, and she knows now that she has a bottom line: "I deserve respect from my children, and anything less than that is accepting abuse from them. I'm not willing to substitute abuse from my children for abuse from my husband."

2. You have the right to

Be heard. You have a voice and opinions and ideas and values. You have a right to say what they are. No one has to agree with you or like what you say. As long as they are yours, they are important and valuable.

> *Charlotte has lived with abuse for many years. She's looking for a counselor, and has tried out three different people.*
>
> *Each one told her what she should do, and her response was, "They're not listening to me. I have my own ideas and opinions, and I don't want to be told what to do. I'll keep on looking until I find a counselor who respects my values."*
>
> *Right on, Charlotte!*

3. You have the right to

Say "No." And to say "No" without giving a reason. It may be easier for you to say "Yes," and you may like saying "Yes" better than saying "No." As long as you know you have the choice to say "No," you are okay. If "Yes" is a knee-jerk reaction to all requests, you are in trouble.

> *Marlene stopped by to visit the other day. She was a shelter resident last year. She said, "I'm dating again, and last week my boyfriend and I were sitting in the car. He suggested a movie that he wanted to see, and I said, 'No, I don't want to see that movie.'*
>
> *"We went to see one that we both liked. It was wonderful! I asserted myself, and I didn't even say why I didn't want to see his movie. I feel great!"*

You have the right to a support system.

4. You have the right to

Have a support system. To put all your eggs in one basket, or to depend emotionally on one other person, is to court disaster. No one other person can meet all your needs. Diversify: get some needs met by a lover, some by family, by friends, by groups. Then when one of your supports disappoints you, you have others to turn to.

> *Freida was a happy, independent woman. After she met and married Carl, he insisted she quit her job. He bought them a house in another state, away from her large, supportive family and her circle of friends.*
>
> *When Freida attempted to get involved in groups in her new community, Carl found ways to embarrass her, and she soon stopped trying. Freida was cut off from all the resources she relied on.*
>
> *Carl's plan of manipulation and control backfired, however. When Freida had no one else to turn to except Carl, she finally saw him clearer than ever before.*
>
> *Freida left Carl, and returned to her family who helped her get her own apartment and a job she enjoys. She is starting to renew friendships and to be social again. Freida says she will always make sure she has a support system for herself, and she won't trust anyone who tries to undermine it.*

5. You have the right to

Come and go as you please. If you don't feel free to go where you want when you want, it's time to look at WHY. See what is self-imposed and what is being imposed on you. *Make choices.*

Sarah thought it strange that Don insisted on bringing her to her group meetings and waiting outside for her. She talked about it at group and was amazed to hear that his behavior was typical of a controlling personality. She began to connect other behaviors of his with this one: he always answered the phone, wouldn't let her drive the car, did the grocery shopping with her, and called her several times during the day to find out what she was doing. On days she wasn't there to receive his calls, he demanded an accounting of her time. Then he accused her of flirting, seeing other men, and cheating on him.

When Sarah stopped feeling responsible for Don's obsessiveness, she realized that she had a right to come and go as she pleased. She saw that Don's complaints and accusations had been controlling her behavior.

Sarah doesn't sit at home by the phone anymore. She doesn't like hearing Don's insults, but they don't stop her from living. She hears them for what they are—attempts to make her act differently from what she knows is normal.

6. You have the right to

Have friends and be social. Studies show that the people most likely to be depressed are those who are raising small children, and who do not work outside the home. It can be an isolating experience.

Take the time "to make new friends and keep the old, one is silver, the other gold," as the song says. Part of you is a social person, and having friends and socializing is important.

For Barbara, taking courses at the local community college was an important part of her social life. She always met new people and was interested in their stories and their lives.

Barbara had been dating Ed for nine months when it was time to register for fall classes. She was surprised to hear Ed put down the school and the expressive dance class she was planning to take. He told her that he wanted them to have "a special night together" once a week, and he picked the evening of her class. He asked, "Which do you care about most, me or the class?"

Barbara felt uneasy, and didn't like the either/or choice Ed was forcing on her. But she dropped the class.

When this was repeated in January over an aerobics class, Barbara again gave in. Over the spring and summer, Barbara felt the loss of her usual social self, and she was determined not to let it happen a third time.

When Barbara signed up for the same dance class she had missed the previous year, Ed came up with another reason she shouldn't take it. "If you care about me, you won't go," he said.

This time Barbara said, "I care about you, and I am going to my class. I care about me, too."

7. You have the right to

Have privacy and space of your own. The need for your own space and for privacy doesn't disappear with marriage and motherhood. It's often given up by women as one of the prices to be paid for having a family. Take it back. Without it you will lose your sense of self and your sense of identity. With it you can maintain an idea of who you are and what you want, and not in relationship to anything or anyone else.

If you want to love others, love yourself first. If you are trying to meet the needs of others without first meeting your own, it's like trying to water plants with an empty pitcher.

Grace was 45 when she married George. She had two teenage daughters, and he had an 18-year-old son who lived with his ex-wife. Grace had been a single mother for 14 years, and she was used to running her household in her own way.

This included keeping her den as her private space where she completed her work as a freelance writer. It was the one room in the house where the girls were not allowed, and they respected their mother's need for privacy.

George, however, had no such notions. When he moved in, he made Grace's den the object of his attention and scrutiny. He browsed over her books and moved them around. He read everything he found, and at dinner would critique her writing. He had opinions about how she should reorganize the den. "It's so messy," he said.

One day when Grace was gone, George moved his easy chair and his collection of pipes into her den. He announced that from now on he would be using it as his "relaxation room."

Grace felt invaded, and couldn't function without her space and privacy. She was torn between her love for Ed and her own needs.

After several months of tormenting herself for being selfish, Grace asked Ed to leave. They date

*now, but Grace is wary of living with Ed again
unless she can be sure it won't mean sacrificing her
own need for privacy.*

8. You have the right to

Maintain a separate identity. For many women, this is
a formidable task. They see themselves only in relation
to someone else: daughter, in relation to mother; sister,
in relation to brother; wife, in relation to husband;
mistress, in relation to lover; secretary, in relation
to boss.

To feel confident enough to tell someone, "No, you
can't beat me. I will leave you."

Or, "No, you can't harass me. I will complain to the
company president."

Or, "No, you can't cheat on me and expect me to
stay."

All these statements require a separate identity—an
identity that will set limits and boundaries about what
behaviors you are willing to accept, and what behaviors
you won't accept. Without it, decisions will be impossible, and a feeling of helplessness, if not hopelessness,
will overcome you.

*When I first met Darlene four years ago, she did
not see herself as a separate person. She described
herself as an abused daughter, a battered wife, and
an inadequate mother.*

*Since then, Darlene has left her abusive hus-
band, gotten a divorce, and resettled in another
state. She has been in and out of shelters and has
been consistent in her quest for good counseling.
She attended Alanon meetings, support groups,*

*Parents Anonymous, family counseling, and indi-
vidual counseling for herself and her son. She
found a Big Brother program for Johnny, and
enrolled him in a mini-bike program that includes
rap sessions.*

*Darlene has her own apartment, and she
recently got a secretarial job with a law firm. Now
she makes over $30,000 a year.*

*Darlene sees herself, not in relation to anyone
else, but first as a person in her own right.*

dreams are lost

all my dreams were dashed the day you hit me
all my hopes were halted by your hate
all my love dissolved in your denials
all my faith faltered by your fist

there are no dreams left for me to give you
i've lost whatever hope of us i had
i have no strength to hold us both together
violence wins again and dreams are lost.

Safety from bodily harm for myself and my children.

To Leave
or
Not to Leave

THREE

By leaving I mean that you're leaving your present situation. That could mean moving out with your children. It could mean moving out without the children. It could mean that you obtain a restraining and vacate order and he leaves. Or it could mean that you both leave the house or apartment.

Reasons to leave:

1. Safety from bodily harm for yourself and your children

2. More self-respect, self-confidence, and a sense of identity

3. Gaining control over your own life

4. Increased peace and tranquility

5. Sense of independence

1. Safety from bodily harm for yourself and your children

It is easier for a woman to make a decision to save her children than it is to make a decision to save herself. If the children are attacked, she can act. If she is hit, she may still stay, thinking it is best for the children because they need a father.

The truth is that she needs to be safe, and the children need to be safe. Everyone needs to be safe. That is the priority. Nothing takes precedence over that. Safety. First. All else comes later.

2. More self-respect, self-confidence, and a sense of identity

Our sense of self-respect in great part comes from the messages we get from those around us. When the message is a beating or verbal abuse, it is hard to maintain one's self-respect.

Self-confidence often comes from the positive reinforcement received from past behavior. When the reinforcement is a beating, it is hard to have self-confidence.

Self-identity comes from the image you have of yourself and the image others have of you. Looking at a swollen face in the mirror or feeling the pain of black and blue bruises doesn't encourage a positive self-identity.

3. Gaining control over your own life

Even though it may feel just the opposite, leaving could be the only way you gain control over your life. It may mean being *temporarily* out of control over where you live, what job you hold, or what schools your children attend.

Anyone who learns to ride a bike, drive a car, or swim feels temporarily out of control. You have to give up one control to gain another. Gaining control over your basic right to physical safety is the priority. Put that first. The others will come later.

4. Increased peace and tranquility

You need and deserve a feeling of being safe, okay, at least content. You need a feeling of well-being, that things are in order, that you don't have to look over your shoulder nor feel like a fugitive. You shouldn't have to walk on egg shells or measure your words.

5. Sense of independence

"I Did It My Way" is the title of an old song. The excitement of doing something your own way is exhilarating. Who cares if you make mistakes? Doing it your way is more important than doing it the "right" way.

Reasons to stay

1. "The unknown is worse than the known."

2. "I can't make it on my own financially."

3. "I'm afraid of being lonely."

4. "I'd have to go to work, and I might fail."

1. "The unknown is worse than the known."

"At least I know what I've got. If I leave, I don't know what I'll have." Fear of the unknown is awesome and immobilizing.

2. "I can't make it on my own financially."

Leaving home will mean many financial adjustments, a different lifestyle.

"I might have to go on welfare, move in with my family, get a job, put the children in day care, sell the house, find an apartment. I hate living with violence and fear, but having no money scares me more."

3. "I'm afraid of being lonely."

"I know what it's like to be unpopular, not having dates, spending Saturday nights alone. He may be violent, but at least he's company."

4. "I'd have to go to work, and I might fail."

"What if no one wants me and I can't find a job? Or what if I find a job and then get fired? I can't take any more rejection."

These reasons for not leaving are real. Any one of them could be the one that keeps you from leaving. Fear is powerful. It can keep you from saving your own life. None of the CONS are worth dying for. Living is the bottom line. It's the number one priority.

There are ways of coping with loneliness, rejection, lack of money, but only if you're alive to do it. Survival comes first. Learning to live with fears comes later.

However, instead of asking "Why does a woman stay in a violent marriage?" we should be asking, "What is it about marriage and society that keeps a woman captive in a violent marriage?"

This question raises an important issue. We won't find the right answers until we begin to ask the right questions. In the meantime . . .

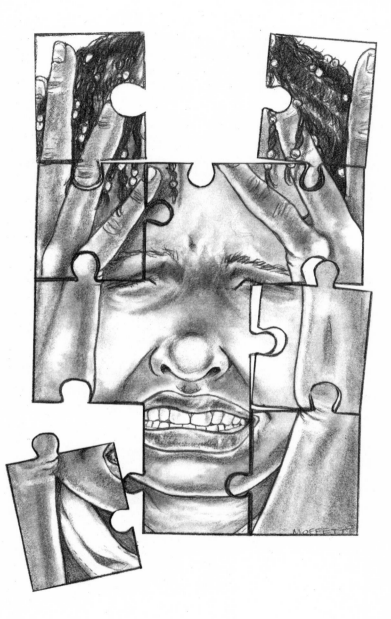

I can't think anymore . . . I've lost me.

loss

I can't think anymore
I used to be able to think.

I can't cry anymore
I used to be able to cry.

I feel empty all the time
I used to feel filled up.

I'm tired all the time
I used to have energy to spare.

I think everything is all my fault
I used to know that it wasn't.

I don't feel things anymore
I used to feel shocked.

I won't tell myself what I'm feeling
I used to share my feelings with friends.

I'm a stranger to myself
I've lost me.

quietly

quietly i accept

> without bands or
> fanfare or
> bugles or
> flag waving

quietly i accept

> who i am
> who you are
> what i do not do
> what you do

quietly i am

> passive
> helpless
> hopeless
> desperate
> lonely
> endangered

quietly.

"I Can't Leave Because . . . "

You may be telling yourself things that make you stay:

1. "He can't live without me."

2. "The children need a father."

3. "He'll kill me if I go."

4. "I can't make it alone."

5. "I have no education, no skills."

6. "It's going to get better."

7. "No one believes me."

8. "I'll lose my kids."

9. "I can't give up my dream of a good marriage."

10. "My mother says to stay."

1. "He can't live without me."

Often the man instills in the woman the notion that he will have a nervous breakdown, will kill himself, become a hopeless drunk, or lose his job if she leaves.

When asked why she stays and takes the beatings, the abused woman often says, "He needs me."

He says he can't live without you. Ask yourself if you can live without him. If you've been beaten, you can't live with him. Any other information is irrelevant.

Ann is a computer programmer and in her fifties. She divorced her abusive husband five years ago. She had to quit her high-paying job due to cancer surgery, and she now collects disability payments.

Ann's abusive boyfriend of three years is alcoholic and unemployed. Every time Ann made attempts to leave him, he said, "I'll commit suicide if you leave me. I can't live without you. I love you more than anyone else ever will."

This was especially difficult for Ann because her daughter had committed suicide when she was 17.

Through group work and individual sessions, Ann was able to work through the feelings of loss over her daughter's death. She came to realize that she did not make her daughter die, and that if she left her boyfriend, it was not her responsibility to decide what he would do.

Ann moved into her own apartment and is now getting involved in volunteer work. (Her ex-boyfriend is still alive.)

2. "The children need a father."

There's one thing the children need more than an abusive father, and that's a living mother. You aren't any good to them bruised and broken.

A peaceful single mother is worth more than a violent father and mother. Our violent society teaches our children by war, competitive sports, violence on television and on the streets that men should be powerful, women weak, that men should dominate, women give in. They are handed a pattern of power to shape their future lives.

By rejecting violence in our personal relationships, in our communications with our friends and neighbors, in our response to our leaders and to our government, we can teach our children a new model of non-violence. Rejecting an abusive father may be the first step.

Every time Joan took her two children and left her abusive husband, her family beseeched her to return to him because "the children need a father."

He, too, called her and said, "I miss the girls; you can't stop me from seeing them. I have a right to help raise them; they need a father."

Joan was emotionally torn. She agreed with her family and her abuser: she wanted her girls to have a father. But she also knew that they didn't need an abusive father.

At a single parents meeting, Joan met a gentle

man whom she is dating. He is encouraging her to
say "No" to returning to abuse.

Joan arranges for her daughters to spend time
with their father, and they also spend time with
Joan's new boyfriend. They are now able to watch
adults interact without the power and control
dynamics they saw in the past.

3. "He'll kill me if I go."

He'll kill you if you stay.

Diana thought she knew her boyfriend of six
months pretty well. Then one night he came over to
her apartment and she got the shock of her life. He
told her that he was a professional murderer.

He held a knife to her throat and said he would
kill her if she ever told anyone or if she ever left
him. Then he took the knife and continually cut
himself all over both his arms, spilling blood all
over the kitchen, all over himself, and all over
Diana. Then he left.

Diana was in shock until morning. Then, with
the help of friends, she called the police and got a
restraining order. Her boyfriend was picked up,
taken to the hospital, given a psychological evalua-
tion, and taken to jail. Diana has left her job and
her apartment, and has moved to another commu-
nity. She doesn't want him to be able to find her
when he's released from jail.

Diana is doing all the right things to protect
herself.

John's message to her was, "I'll kill you if you
leave me." She left anyway.

fear

it descends upon me like a cloud

hovers me

covers me

the cloud follows me everywhere

goes to bed with me

wakes up with me

eats with me

drives with me

shops with me
I wait for the cloud to disappear

4. "I can't make it alone."

Maybe not. And you'll never know if you don't try.
You're not as alone as you may think. There are over
twenty-eight million abused women in the United States.
One out of every two wives is abused.

All over this country shelters are springing up to
house you. Support groups are forming so you have a
place to talk. Counselors are available to talk over
issues. Legal advocates will go to court with you. The
women of the world are responding to domestic
violence.

You may not make it alone—but know that you are
not alone.

> *We have counseled with Pam for over a year.*
> *She has lived with violence from her first husband,*
> *divorced him, and now lives with a violent*
> *boyfriend.*
>
> *Pam prides herself on being in control in an*
> *atmosphere that is uncontrollable. She really*
> *believes he can't get along without her, so she*
> *chooses to live in an explosive situation.*
>
> *I worry about Pam. Her chances of getting*
> *killed are high. She is choosing a dangerous*
> *tightrope to walk.*
>
> *She really believes that she is in control, and she*
> *is living with a man who cannot control his own*
> *behavior. She hopes he will get counseling at*
> *Emerge, a counseling agency for men who are*
> *abusive.*
>
> *In the meantime, Pam says, "I'm staying*
> *because he needs me."*

5. "I have no education, no skills."

Will you have any more by staying? Or will leaving motivate you to do something you've always wanted to do anyway but never could force yourself to do? Take a typing course, learn to drive a car, enroll in school. You know more than you give yourself credit for.

> *Carol married while she was still in high school because she was pregnant. Six years, two children, and two abusive husbands later, she came in for counseling.*
>
> *"What's wrong with me?" she asked. "I feel like I'm going crazy. I didn't finish high school, I've never held a job, and I don't think I can make it by myself.*
>
> *"Without a man, I feel like half a person, and I need someone to help me raise the children. So I feel like I have to go back to my first husband or live with the second, and both of them are abusive and violent. I don't know what to do. I feel like I'm going crazy."*

What Carol is experiencing is common to women who are making new decisions. It is lonely, and it is scary. It takes time to get some training, some education, a job, and new friends to help with the parental responsibilities. You need to be patient with yourself while you explore new horizons and allow yourself to feel a little scared.

6. "It's going to get better."

Hope springs eternal in the human breast, and the hope that he will change is a powerful hope. *The only way it's going to get better is if you change.* Without change on your part, you can be sure it will get worse.

Many women have told me they want their lives to be better. When I ask them what they are willing to do to change it, their honesty is disarming:

> *"Nothing," Claire said. "Well, I don't want to do anything, I just want things to get better. I keep hoping they will."*
>
> *This kind of passive hope is the subject of the book,* **The Cinderella Syndrome.** *The fairy tale Cinderella taught us that if we work hard, a handsome prince will find us and take us to his castle to live happily ever after. This tale encourages women to be passive, to hope, to wait; not to act, and not to make decisions.*
>
> *For women who are living with violence, however, hope is not enough. A clear picture of reality, as it is, not as you want it to be, is healthier and safer.*
>
> *But you have to give up the Cinderella fantasy, and that may be your first step toward reality.*

7. "No one believes me."

"No one believes that he would do this to me. People like him. They think I'm exaggerating."

You are not exaggerating, and there are lots of people to talk to who will believe you. Be selective in who you choose to talk with. Choose people who will understand.

> *When Janice came in to talk, she was still in a state of shock. Her boyfriend of seven years became*

enraged one night and brutally beat her for three hours. She saved herself by holding a pillow over her head.

"I knew he would kill me if I let go of the pillow," she said. "I held onto it, and he couldn't get it away from me."

Janice admitted herself to the hospital under an assumed name because she was so ashamed. She didn't want anyone to know who she was. Her face was swollen, and her eyes were black, so she called in sick at the office for several days.

The few people she talked with on the phone didn't believe her. "Jim would never do a thing like that," she heard friends tell her. She started to feel crazy, and question if it had really happened. The bruises she saw when she looked in the mirror reminded her that it was true.

Janice called us in desperate need to be heard and to be believed. She used her assumed name, still fearing that her family might find out what had happened.

When I mentioned her legal options of pressing charges against Jim, she said, "I just need to talk; I just want to be heard and to be believed. I can't go to court because I don't want my name in the paper."

Janice came to talk for several weeks. She has left Jim, and she is starting to date again. Some close friends have been supportive, and she is getting the understanding and nurturing she needs so badly.

I think she is still trying to understand how a man she thought she knew, a man who was kind,

*loving, and caring for seven years, could suddenly
lash out at her and almost kill her.*

8. "I'll lose my kids."

"If I leave, he'll take the kids away from me. He can
afford lawyers. He'll lie. He'll kidnap them. He'd do
anything to get at me. If I leave, he'll get at me through
the kids. I have to stay if I want to keep my children."
You're no good to the children dead.

*Margaret has two teenage girls, and was mar-
ried for seventeen years to an alcoholic husband.
She said, "He'd go to my job on payday and pick
up my check. By the time I got home, he had cashed
it and bought booze, and he was out drinking.*

*"Many times the refrigerator was empty, and
there was no food in the house. The girls would
need school clothes, and I couldn't buy them.*

*"I'm a nurse, and all the money I earned he
stole for drinking. We were evicted from apart-
ments because of his loud fits of anger and
throwing furniture around.*

*"He'd beat me up when he ran out of alcohol,
and I took it all—until he hit the girls.*

*"That did it. The night he hit them, I took them
to the hospital, packed up our things, and we left
for good.*

*"We'll never go back. I could take all that abuse
myself, but when he hit them, I got bullshit, and it
was all over."*

*Margaret has moved to a new community, and
has a live-in nursing job. She is saving money so
she can afford an apartment. Then she can get the
girls out of foster care to live with her again.*

9. "I can't give up my dream of a good marriage."

"It's what I've always wanted. I don't want to fail."

It's time for a new dream. A dream of no beatings, no harassment, of dignity and self-worth. That dream is better than the reality of a violent marriage.

"Dreams die hard," Sandra said. "I've been conditioned since I was a little girl that the most important thing is a good marriage. I'm beginning to think it meant that any marriage is the most important thing.

"I wonder if there are any good marriages? I'm on my third, and it's not much better than the first two.

"The first man was alcoholic and a compulsive gambler, the second was abusive and a womanizer. The man I'm married to now is a homosexual. I have no problem with that, except that he's married to me.

"We're in couples counseling now, and I hope it will lead to a separation or a divorce. I'm finally ready to give up on this dream of an ideal marriage. I think I'd just like to be in a healthy relationship for awhile."

10. "My mother says to stay."

"When I told my mother about the abuse I was getting, she said, 'I put up with it, and you can too.'"

When Alice came in, she said, "I played out my mother's dream for me: to be married and have a family. I did it for years. I had two children, and when my husband started being abusive, I went to my mother.

"You know what she said? She said, 'So what? I've lived with your alcoholic father for forty years, and I put up with the abuse. So can you.' That's what she said.

"I couldn't believe it. She told me to stop complaining and go home to my husband where I belonged. 'That's all women can expect from a man.' My own mother. I wish she would have told me to leave him."

i can live with a whisper

i will swoop you into the folds of my being

i will encompass you as you encompass me

i will engulf you, smother you

and your voice will become quiet

it will withdraw to a whisper

it will grow peaceful

I will listen to the pounding of my own heartbeat

and it will drown you out

i will mother myself

and your voice will become a whisper

i can live with a whisper

If I could give you up . . . If . . .

If

If I could give you up
I could
> go on with my life
> protect my children
> get a job
> have friends
> laugh

If I could give you up
I could
> leave the dishes in the sink
> talk on the phone at night
> watch romantic movies on TV
> skip dinner
> have no beer in the refrigerator

If I could give you up
If.

when i left you

the day i forgave you your abuse of me
that moment when i said, "i love you still"
the very second i saw through you
into peacefulness
that's when i left you and became free

it wasn't when you were hitting me
nor when you woke me in the night
not when you broke the kitchen table
or even when you infringed upon my rights

it was after.

when you cried and said you'd change
and i knew you couldn't even if you tried
i saw you and saw through you
into peacefulness

that's when i left you and became free.

Getting a Perspective on Violence

FIVE

Things to remember:

1. You did not cause the attack.

2. You cannot keep it from happening again.

3. Your words/actions do not influence his.

4. Alcohol does not cause violence— it is the excuse he uses to be violent.

5. Because he is sorry afterward doesn't excuse what he did.

6. You are not one of his possessions to be used as he sees fit.

7. He is not "king of his castle." If the king is abusive, he needs to be dethroned.

8. Whatever he does in the privacy of his home is not okay. What is done in the privacy of the home must be agreeable with both people. Otherwise, it's time to "go public."

9. You don't deserve to be beaten.

10. You are not to blame for the violence. Look elsewhere to place the blame.

11. You cannot control his violence. You are powerless to control it. You are free to manage your own life.

disbelief

i can't believe you did this

to the one you say you love

i don't know what came over you

that made you push and shove

you're not the man i care about

the one i love and know

who is this monster maniac

where did my lover go?

i can't believe you did this

i can't believe you

i can't believe

i can't.

I am going to leave you

When was it I decided I would leave you?
When was it that I knew our love was lost?
When was it hope eluded dreams of us-ness?
When was it I awoke and knew the cost?

Ten years ago I decided I would leave you
Ten years ago I knew our love was lost
Ten years ago hope eluded dreams of us-ness
Ten years ago I awoke and knew the cost

One of these days I'm going to leave you.

Lesbian
Battering

SIX

The text and stories in most of this book are written about women who have been battered by men. These words are for the victims who are battered by other women. Every year thousands of women are being abused by their female partners.

Abuse is not confined to heterosexual relationships.

"Lesbian battering is that pattern of violent and coercive behaviors whereby a lesbian seeks to control the thoughts, beliefs or conduct of her intimate partner or to punish the intimate for resisting the perpetrator's control over her . . . it is the pattern of intimidation, coercion, terrorism or violence, the sum of all past acts of violence and the promises of future violence, that achieves enhanced power and control for the perpetrator over her partner." (Seal Press: *Naming the Violence*, pp. 173-174.)

Women abuse women. The abuse of women in same-sex relationships is just as painful, hurtful, harmful, and dangerous as any other abuse. Many women report that it is worse because of the shock that it is another woman inflicting it.

> *Jane joined the support group for battered lesbians and told of the terror she lives with. "Nothing I do is right; I'm constantly criticized, put-down, or ignored. My lover accuses me of sleeping with other women, and nothing I say changes her mind.*
>
> *"Two years ago I told her I couldn't take it anymore, and I was leaving. She beat me up. Then she held me and comforted me, and told me she only did it because she is in so much pain herself.*
>
> *"You know what? I bought it! I ended up feeling sorry for her. Can you believe it? For her. And she's the one who hit me.*
>
> *"I'm afraid to leave her. For myself and for her. She says she'll commit suicide. And if I left and she didn't do herself in, I think she'd find me no matter where I went. I'm afraid to stay, and I'm afraid to leave. I'm always afraid."*

It is not safe for many lesbians to disclose their sexual preference. Harassment by family or neighbors, the possible loss of their employment, housing, or possible loss of their natural, adopted, or foster children are threats to their safety, their freedom, and their well being. These are a few of the reasons lesbians fear to disclose that they are being abused by their lovers.

It is not easy, and often it is not even safe, for a battered lesbian to use the legal system to obtain a restraining order or a vacate order to keep her abuser from attacking. In some states, it is not possible for a lesbian to obtain a restraining order. Some judges won't issue them, or they will issue only mutual orders. Some police officers won't enforce them.

Many times the women are fearful that they will not be believed. They fear the abuser will accuse the victim of abuse, and then she is in a "It's my word against yours" situation.

A woman called the hotline. She said she was an attorney, and she was being battered by her female lover. We talked for a long time. I encouraged her to come for counseling and to attend the support group for battered lesbians.

She asked many questions about where we were located, the visibility of the office, if it was held in daytime or if it would be dark outside, and how confidential her identity would be if she joined the group.

After awhile she said she wouldn't be able to get help from us. She just didn't feel safe. She might be seen coming into or leaving our office, and worse than that, there might be someone in the group who knew her or her abusive lover.

She was so frightened she couldn't even tell me about her abuse. I hope she was able to get the help she needed to leave her abuser and be safe.

Because it is so difficult to join a support group, to find an environment free of homophobia, and to be assured of confidentiality, many abused lesbians cannot get the help they need. Because many lesbians in the Women's Movement deny that same sex assaults take place, victims are often met with denials when they seek help. Sometimes abusers themselves are in the helping professions and help perpetuate the denials that abuse has occured.

Are my children paying a price?

Asking the Right Questions

SEVEN

Often women who have lived so long with violence ask the questions, "Why did I put up with it so long? What is wrong with *me*?"

And I say, "Maybe it isn't *you*. Why are you so hard on yourself? You did the best you could with what you knew, and with the resources you had."

That's all you can ask of yourself—to do the best you can. To look at where you are now and reproach yourself for not acting sooner is hindsight, and hindsight distorts herstory.

To understand fully why you didn't make different choices, you would have to go back in time and experience fully the whole situation again. The blame is not yours.

To blame yourself will only keep you from moving forward and keep you from being the fullest, free-est person you are capable of being. That, I think, is the best goal—to be as fully human as you can be—to live without violence, without fear, to have your basic human needs met—food, clothing, shelter, transportation, health, and means of making a living.

You have a right to these. You have the right to question any society that does not provide them, to question any society that encourages violence of any kind.

I suggest to you that instead of asking the question, "What is wrong with *me*?" you ask instead, "What is wrong with the society I live in?" Women who have been victims for so long may not have the answers, but at least we can begin by asking the right questions.

Questions to Ask Yourself

What do I gain by staying in a violent home?

What do my children gain by growing up in
a violent home?

What do I have to lose by leaving?

What do the children have to lose by leaving?

What do I have to gain by leaving?

What do the children have to gain by leaving?

Who can I talk to about my problem?

What are my bottom line expectations for
the future?

What am I willing to live without for the rest of
my life?

What price am I paying for "peace"?

Is it too high?

How long have I been paying it?

Are my children paying a price?

Is it too high?

*How will it affect them five years
from now?*

Without change, what will I be like five years
from now?

What do I want?

How can I get it?

What am I willing to do to get it?

Rise Up Angry

we have been sleeping bears
and we have been roused
we will not sleep again
until our world is no longer
at war with itself.

and the bear is angry
we will raise havoc with injustice
as we see now clearer and clearer
with eyes that are no longer sleepy
we will call upon the goddesses
we will react with the rage of the
mother bear and will protect
the victim, the innocent, the young and the old

those who are responsible will shudder
from the wrath of this mother bear
and will change their ways

we are not vulnerable
we are strong
we are not divided
we are together
we are not alone
we are united

we are not one mother bear
we are a herd of bear
we are strong
we are invincible
and we rise up angry.

Taking Care of Yourself

EIGHT ————————————————————————

At the time of this writing, there have been no giant strides on the part of society to put an end to crimes of violence. Until all of our institutions—political, academic, legal, and others—acknowledge their part in the power struggle, violence will continue its rampant rage.

We cannot force other people or institutions to change; they will have to take on that responsibility themselves. For ourselves, we can admit that we live in an unsafe environment. Our streets, our schools, our courts, even our homes are not safe. We must take care of ourselves and make our own homes, our own environments as safe as possible.

We will wait for others to come to their senses and give up the power game and their senseless need to violate. And in the meantime, we can try to ensure our own physical safety and survival. Here are a few ways to take care of yourself:

1. Remove yourself from the cause of the harm.

If you're swimming in the ocean and a shark appears, you are now in an environment of harm. You can:

- call for help
- hope the shark doesn't notice you
- wish that sharks didn't eat people
- try to outswim the shark
- try to talk the shark out of eating you.

Once you know that the shark is there, you cannot *not* be in fear. So, you can learn to adjust to the fear of being with the shark, or you can choose to live without the fear of being harmed by the shark.

To do that, you must get out of the water. Once out of the water, you are now out of the shark's environment. You can sit on the beach without fear of being harmed by the shark.

Choosing to get out of the water is not an easy choice. You have so many reasons and excuses to stay. No one said it would be easy. But anything less that that is absurd . . . ludicrous . . . suicidal.

2. Find a safe environment.

Get out of danger. Go to a safe place: move in with family, friends, or go to a safe house or shelter.

3. Develop a support system.

Spend time finding out who you can trust and depend on: family, friends, church, support groups, consciousness-raising groups, assertiveness training sessions, etc. Work on maintaining contact.

Be a friend. Then when you need a friend, you'll have one. Isolation is your worst enemy. Avoid isolation. At all costs. There is strength in numbers. Try to feel part of a system, a non-violent system that supports you.

4. Stay healthy.

Take good care of yourself. Good food, good rest, lots of fresh air, and walking a lot every day have helped many women feel good about themselves. Be good to yourself . . . you deserve it.

5. Regain your sense of humor.

You used to laugh and find things funny. Look for things that will make you laugh again: books, movies, television shows, people—anything that is funny to you and will make you laugh. Laughter is better medicine than any pills a doctor can prescribe. Work at it. It won't just happen. You have to plan it.

Spend time with people who are up-beat, optimistic, and joyful. Pick friends who can laugh at themselves and who can laugh with you. There is humor on the other side of tragedy, and some people are better than others at finding it. Seek out people who have a good healthy attitude, and they will bring out the best in you.

Try to regain that playfulness you once had. Try to revive it. It isn't dead. It just got lost somewhere. You can find it again if you take the time to look for it.

Try to remember what your sense of humor was like. It's there—just waiting for you to bring it back to life. Laughter can cure the mind and the body. Start laughing again, and you'll start to feel better.

listen

if you will help me . . .
hear my voice
listen to my words
> my heart
> my unspoken shame
> my nameless dreams

listen

please do not give me your
> opinions
> judgments
> advice
> wisdom

listen to
> my silence
> my terror
> my fears
> my anxiety
> my pain

and please do not interrupt while
i am sharing
> my being
> my past
> my present
> my future

if you will help me . . .
hear my voice
listen.

Find a safe environment . . .

Women's Shelter Movement

NINE

The Women's Shelter Movement began in England. In the 1960s the first shelter for battered women and their children opened in California. There are more than 1500 shelters in the United States.

The grassroots shelter movement is similar to the underground railroad of Harriet Tubman. Shelters provide the escape route for tens of thousands of women and children who live with violence and who have no other escape route. Just as oppressed slaves followed the north star to freedom from enslavement, victims of violence seek safe passage from the bondage of fear and abuse.

The Shelter Movement is a moment in herstory—one in which women who have been liberated from this oppression help those who are not. And like the anti-slavery movement, it is continuing to grow until society acknowledges the tragic and devious crime perpetuated against its women and its children.

This Movement has already grown beyond the initial task of providing safe refuge for women and children. In the past two decades, it has made significant strides through coalition building, networking, lobbying for legislation, and institutional changes.

Women everywhere in the world—Iranian women, Latin American women, Saudi women, European women, Asian women, Native American women, and African women are joining in peace movements. To-gether we are raising one voice: *the violence must end.*

As an outgrowth of the anti-slavery, suffragette, civil rights, and the women's movements, the Shelter Move-ment has accepted the challenge that none of us is free from abuse, from racial bigotry, from homophobia, from economic inequality, from institutional, housing, and employment discrimination, and from crimes against all people until *we all are.*

peace

Be with me in peace
Or go away
It is your in and out
That drives me wild
It's wearing me down

Your changing:
Being there
Going away
Loving me then
Hitting me
Then loving me again

Is wearing me down
Eroding my spirit
Changing me
So I am no longer
Me.

Please be with me in
peace
Or go away
Or I will

Let's have a celebration!

poem of celebration

Let's have a celebration
Let's have a party in the street
Let's dance and sing and laugh a lot
And say good-bye to grief.

We lived a life of fearfulness
A life of broken dreams
It's time to put away the past
Of lies and cheats and schemes.

Our future is before us
A path of work and peace
Women helping women
So war and crime will cease.

We are women in a movement
Saying no to power and might
Singing a celebration
Sharing our delight.

About the Author and Illustrator

Mary Marecek was born and raised in New Hampshire. After teaching elementary school for ten years, she attended the George Warren Brown School of Social Work in St. Louis, and is a psychotherapist.

She worked with the Battered Women's Movement for many years, and was Program Director of Respond. Respond is a shelter and counseling agency in Massachusetts for battered women and their children.

Mary enjoys gardening, golf, crossword puzzles, opera and baseball. She lives and writes in Florida.

Jami Moffett worked as a sign and display artist for ten years before her children were born. She now is a free lance artist in Seattle, Washington. She has created numerous magazine illustrations, but this is her first book.

"I've enjoyed working on this project, and hope my drawings coupled with the text will bring hope and safety to many," she commented.

Jami and her husband, Robert, have three children, Alexandra, 8, Cale, 6, and Markéll, 4.

Bibliography

Betancourt, Marian. *What to Do When Love Turns Violent: A Practical Resource for Women in Abusive Relationships.* 1997. 262 pp. Paper, $12. HarperPerennial< HarperCollins Publishers, Inc., 10 East 53rd STreet, New York, NY 10022.
The first part presents an action plan to get out of danger and find immediate help — making a protective order work, calling the police, finding safe shelter, seeking medical attention, pressing charges, and getting financial assistance. The second part suggests how to stay safe and regain control over a new life. Offers detailed information to help abused women.

Brewster, Susan, M.S.W. *To be an Anchor in the Storm: A Guide for Families and Friends of Abused Women.* 1997. 245 pp. Paper, $12.95. Ballantine Books

Provides guidance for people who want to help a friend or other loved one in her struggle to escape domestic violence. Helps read learn how to recognize the signs of abuse, handle one's own negative feelings, become an effective advocate, and deal with the batterer.

Brown, Lou, Francois Dubau, and Merritt McKeon, J.D. ***Stop Domestic Violence: An Action Plan for Saving Lives.*** 1997. 207 pp. Paper, $11.95; hardcover, St. Martin's Griffin, New York.
Book offers hope and practical strategies for combating domestic viiolence. The first healf is aimed at support network people — parents, families, friends, both personal and professional. The second half offers an action plan for battered women and those around them.

Creighton, Allan, and Paul Kivel. ***Helping Teens Stop Violence: A Practical Guide for Counselors, Educators, and Parents.*** 1992.154 pp. Hunter House, P.O. Box 2914, Alameda, CA 94501-0914. 510/865-5282.
Book is designed to help reader gaini an understanding of the roots of violence in society, and offers steps to follow when helping teens who have been abused. It also provides guidelines for adults setting up teen support groups.

Levy, Barrier, and Patricia Occhiuzzo Giggans. ***What Parents Need to Know about Dating Violence.*** 1995. 172 pp. $12.95. Seal Press. 3131 Western Avenue, Suite 410, Seattle, WA 98121
A book for parents concerned about teenagers in abusive dating relationships. Book gives streaightforward advice to parents, drawing on the real-life experiences of parents and teens as well as the authors' own professional experience.

NiCarthy, Ginny M.S.W. ***Getting Free: You Can End Abuse and Take Back Your Life.*** 1997. 320 pp. $12.95. Seal Press.
Book includes special exercises designed to help reader recognize abuse, gain self-esteem, and decide what she wants from a relationship. Offers gidance and support for building a new life free of abuse.

Reynolds, Marilyn. ***Baby Help.* True-to-Life Series from Hamilton High.** Novel. 1998. 224 pp. Paper, $8.95; hardcover, $15.95 each. Morning Glory Press.
Melissa doesn't consider herself abused — after all, Rudy only hits her occasionally when he's drinking . . . until she realizes the effect his abuse is having on their child.

Sousa, Carole, ed. ***Preventing Teen Dating Violence: A Five-Session Curriculum for Teaching Adolescents.*** 1996. $50. ***Respect Can't Be Beat: Peer Leader's Manual.*** 1995. $15. Dating Violence, Intervention Project, Transition House, P.O. 530, Harvard Square Station, Cambridge, MA 02238. 617/354-2676.
Good resource for teaching both sexes that violence in a relationship is not acceptable.

Videos

"The Children Are Watching." 12 min. $295. AGC, 1560
Sherman Ave., Ste. 100, Evanston, IL 60201.
800/421-2363.
*Focuses on the devastating effects that domestic violence has on
children. Children share their terrifying memories and discuss
the feelings they have around these experiences. Can help teens
understand the devastating effects on the child when daddy
abuses mom.*

"Heart on a Chain: The Truth About Dating Violence." 17
min. $79. Phoenix Learning Group, Inc., 2349 Chaffee
Drive, St. Louis, MO 63146. 314/569-0211.
*Portrays three young men and their attitudes about physical and
emotional abuse in their relationships with their girlfriends.
Abuse is defined as a control issue that involves a violation of
another person that hurts both the victim and the abuser.*

"When Dating Turns Dangerous." 33 min. $99.95. Sunburst
Communications, 101 Castleton St., Pleasantville, NY
10570. 800/431-1934.
*Viewers watch a teen's relationship develop from the first time
her boyfriend hits her on through the escalation of the violence.
Periodically, discussion questions appear on the screen to
encourage viewers to discuss concepts such as, "Is it the
woman's role to keep him happy?" "Is his jealousy a sign of how
much he loves her?" Finally, after her boyfriend beats her so
savagely she is hospitalized, she joins a women's support group.
Comments from participants demonstrate the realities of partner
abuse, and the fact that, once started, the violence usually
escalates. Includes a teacher's guide.*

**For information about shelter services near you,
contact:**

The National Coalition Against Domestic Violence
2401 Virginia Avenue, N.W., Suite 306
Washington, DC 20037
202/293-8860

Index

MORNING GLORY PRESS

6595 San Haroldo Way, Buena Park, CA 90620-3748
714/828-1998; 888/612-8254 — FAX 714/828-2049; 888/327-4362

ORDER FORM

Please send me the following: Price   Total

Breaking Free from Partner Abuse

___   Paper 1-885356-53-6   8.95   _____

Novels by Marilyn Reynolds:

___   *Baby Help*   1-885356-27-7   8.95   _____
___   *But What About Me?*   1-885356-10-2   8.95   _____
___   *Too Soon for Jeff*   0-930934-91-1   8.95   _____
___   *Detour for Emmy*   0-930934-76-8   8.95   _____
___   *Telling*   1-885356-03-x   8.95   _____
___   *Beyond Dreams*   1-885356-00-5 •   8.95   _____
___ *Do I Have a Daddy?*   Paper 0-930934-44-x   5.95   _____

___   Hardcover 0-930934-45-8   12.95   _____
___ *¿Yo tengo papá?*   Paper 0-930934-82-2   5.95   _____
                                       Hardcover 0-930934-83-0   12.95   _____

Parents, Pregnant Teens, Adoption Option

___   Paper 0-930934-28-8   8.95   _____

Pregnant? Adoption Is an Option.

___   Paper 1-885356-08-0   11.95   _____
___ *Surviving Teen Pregnancy* Paper 1-885356-06-4   11.95   _____

School-Age Parents: Three-Generation Living

___   Paper 0-930934-36-9   10.95   _____

Teen Moms: The Pain and the Promise

___   Paper, 1-885356-25-0   14.95   _____

___   Hardcover 1-885356-24-2   21.95   _____

Teenage Couples: Expectations and Reality

___   Paper 0-930934-98-9   14.95   _____
___   Hardcover 0-930934-99-7   21.95   _____
        — *Caring, Commitment and Change*
___   Paper 0-930934-93-8   9.95   _____
___   Hardcover 0-930934-92-x   15.95   _____
        — *Coping with Reality*
___   Paper 0-930934-86-5   9.95   _____
___   Hardcover 0-930934-87-3   15.95   _____
___ *Will the Dollars Stretch?* Paper 1-885356-12-9   6.95   _____
___   Teacher's Guide 1-885356-15-3   2.50   _____

TOTAL   _____

Please add postage: 10% of total—Min., $3.50;
15%, Outside U.S.   _____
California residents add 7.75% sales tax   _____

TOTAL   _____

Ask about quantity discounts, Teacher, Student Guides.
Prepayment requested. School/library purchase orders accepted.
If not satisfied, return in 15 days for refund.

NAME _____ PHONE_____
ADDRESS _____
_____